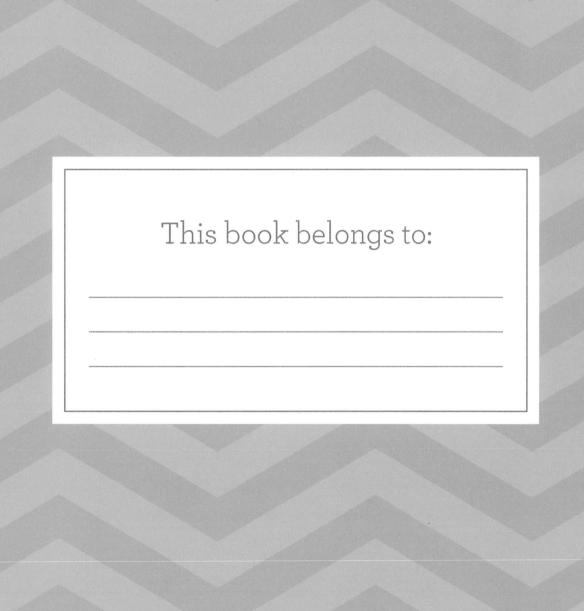

This book belongs to:

_____

_____

_____

Let your story, your tale begin

with this book of fond memories

of all that you've been

and our hopes and our dreams

for all that you'll be.

WELCOME LITTLE ONE

A Keepsake Baby Book

KRISTIN BAIRD RATTINI

NATIONAL GEOGRAPHIC

WASHINGTON, D.C.

To Emily, my little one always

Since 1888, the National Geographic Society has funded more than 12,000 research, exploration, and preservation projects around the world. National Geographic Partners distributes a portion of the funds it receives from your purchase to National Geographic Society to support programs including the conservation of animals and their habitats.

National Geographic Partners
1145 17th Street NW
Washington, DC 20036-4688 USA

Become a member of National Geographic and activate your benefits today at natgeo.com/jointoday.

For information about special discounts for bulk purchases, please contact National Geographic Books Special Sales: specialsales@natgeo.com

For rights or permissions inquiries, please contact National Geographic Books Subsidiary Rights: bookrights@natgeo.com

ISBN: 978-1-4262-1895-8

Interior design: Callie Strobel

Printed in China

17/RRDS/1

CONTENTS

YOU'RE HERE

· · · · · · · · · · ·

There's no more waiting;

at last, you're here!

There's so much about you

to love, to behold, and to share.

FAMILY TREE

Me:

_____

Sisters: Brothers:

_____   _____

_____   _____

Parents:

_____

Grandparents:

_____

_____

Grandparents:

_____

_____

"The family is one of nature's masterpieces."

—GEORGE SANTAYANA

YOUR PARENTS

{insert photo here}

{insert photo here}

Full name:

_____

Also known as:

_____

Birth date:

_____

Hometown:

_____

Current job:

_____

Favorite things:

_____

_____

_____

Full name:

_____

Also known as:

_____

Birth date:

_____

Hometown:

_____

Current job:

_____

Favorite things:

_____

_____

_____

"The best thing to hold onto in life is each other."

—AUDREY HEPBURN

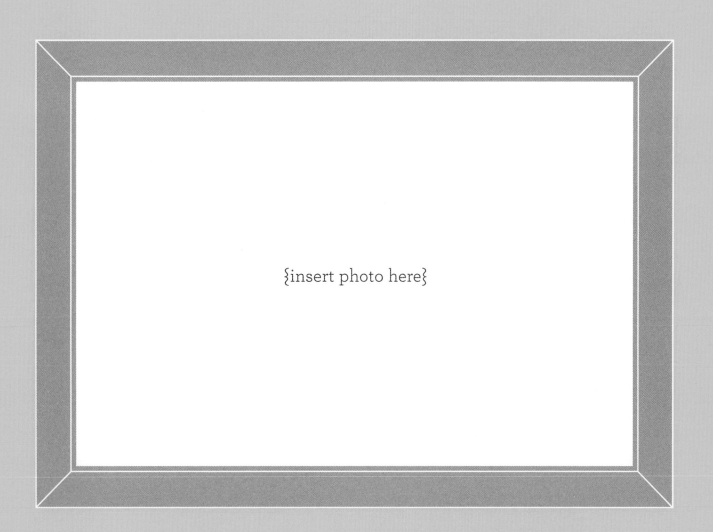

{insert photo here}

"Love recognizes no barriers.
It jumps hurdles,
leaps fences,
penetrates walls to arrive
at its destination
full of hope."

—MAYA ANGELOU

YOUR GRANDPARENTS

Full names:

_____

_____

_____

_____

You call them:

_____

_____

_____

_____

Where they live:

_____

_____

Full names:

_____

_____

_____

_____

You call them:

_____

_____

_____

_____

Where they live:

_____

_____

"Nobody gets to live
life backward.
Look ahead,
that is where
your future lies."

-ANN LANDERS

GETTING READY

This ultrasound photo of you was taken:

_____

Your mom was _____ weeks pregnant.

How we felt when we saw you:

_____

_____

_____

_____

_____

_____

_____

{insert photo here}

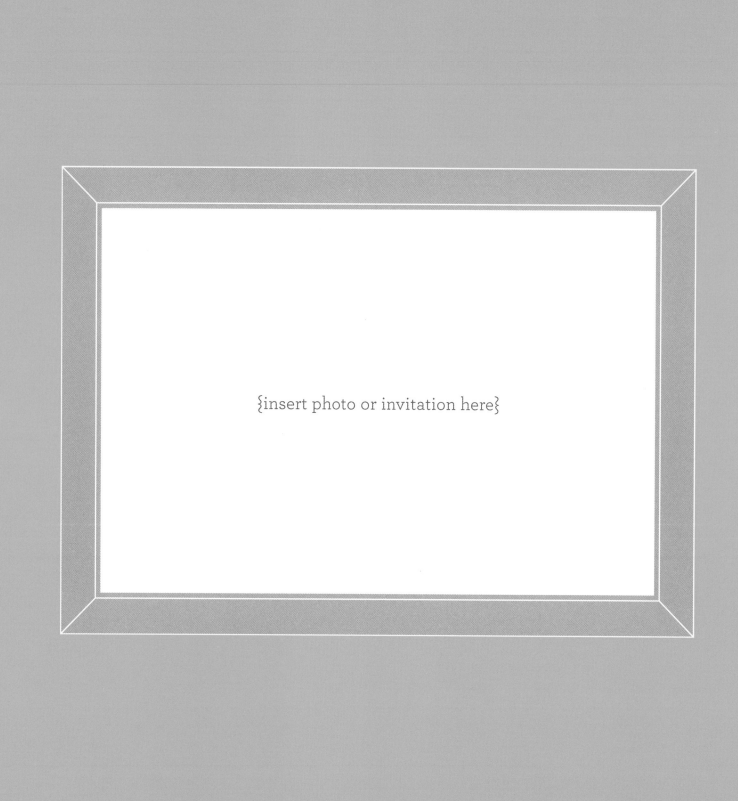

{insert photo or invitation here}

SHOWERED WITH LOVE

Your baby shower was held:

_____

It was hosted by:

_____

Family and friends who shared in the excitement:

_____

_____

Some of the thoughtful gifts you received:

_____

_____

_____

_____

"Today a new sun rises for me; everything lives, everything is animated, everything seems to speak to me of my passion, everything invites me to cherish it."

—NINON DE LENCLOS

GRAND ENTRANCE

Your due date:

_____

You arrived on: _____ at: _____

Place of birth: Weight and length:

_____   _____

Your doctor:

_____

Lasting memory of your delivery:

_____

_____

_____

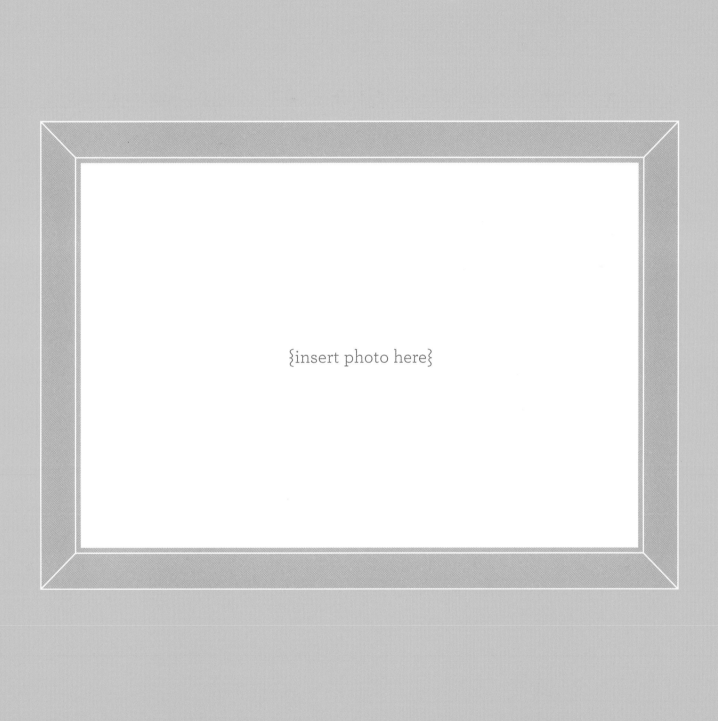
{insert photo here}

GETTING TO KNOW YOU

Your full name is:

_____

We chose your name because:

_____

_____

We also like to call you:

_____

Other names we considered:

_____

_____

_____

How Babies Around the World Get Their Names

On the Indonesian island of Bali, children are named according to their birth order.

In Nigeria, babies born in the Yoruba community receive two names. One describes the circumstances of the birth (in the rainy season or hot weather). The other is a hope for the baby's future (long life, endless happiness).

Many Indian parents consult astrological charts and choose their child's name based on his or her birth star.

In Greece, a firstborn boy is traditionally named for his paternal grandfather, a firstborn girl for her paternal grandmother.

> "There is a sun within
> every person."
>
> —RUMI

Your eyes are the color:

_____

Your hair is the color:

_____

Your most distinguishing features are:

_____

_____

_____

You seem to resemble:

_____

_____

_____

{insert photo here}

YOUR HOMECOMING

The date you came home:

_____

Your home address:

_____

_____

Your nursery's theme:

_____

What you wore:

_____

Memories from your first day at home:

_____

"You are built not to shrink down to less, but to blossom into more. To be more splendid. To be more extraordinary. To use every moment to fill yourself up."

— OPRAH WINFREY

WHEN YOU WERE BORN

World headlines:

_____

_____

Popular songs:

_____

_____

World leaders and famous celebrities:

_____

_____

Price of a gallon of milk: _____

Price of a gallon of gasoline: _____

"The world of the future is in our making. Tomorrow is now."

—ELEANOR ROOSEVELT

BRINGING YOU HOME

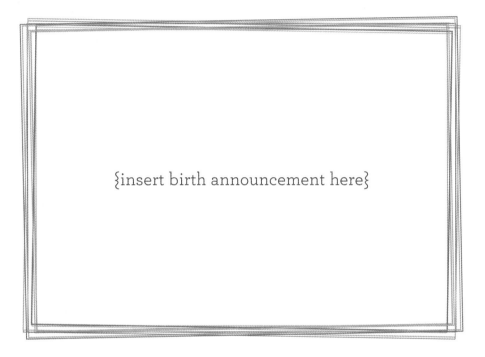

{insert birth announcement here}

We celebrated your arrival by:

_____

_____

Friends and family who helped us celebrate:

_____

_____

Bringing Home Baby
Around the World

In China, at the "full moon" celebration marking a child's first month of life, parents give friends and relatives red-dyed eggs, which represent fertility and good luck.

At the Egyptian Sebou ceremony celebrated on a baby's seventh day, guests make loud noises to build the baby's character and make the child brave.

In Jamaica, a baby's umbilical cord is buried and a tree is planted over it to celebrate the beginning of the child's life.

Aboriginal babies in Australia are briefly held over a smoking pit of green emu bush leaves. The smoke is thought to make the baby healthier and stronger.

In the Muslim faith, a baby's head is shaved at the Aqiqah, or welcoming ceremony, on the seventh day after birth.

GUESTS & GIFTS

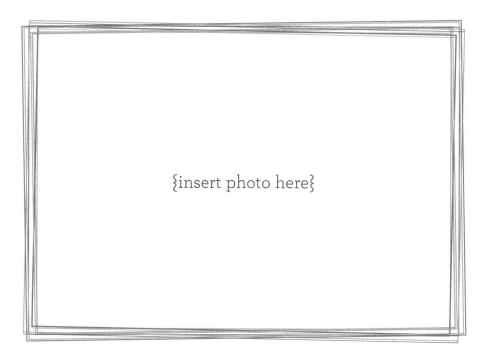

{insert photo here}

Our friends and family couldn't wait to meet you. Some of your visitors were:

_____

_____

_____

_____

_____

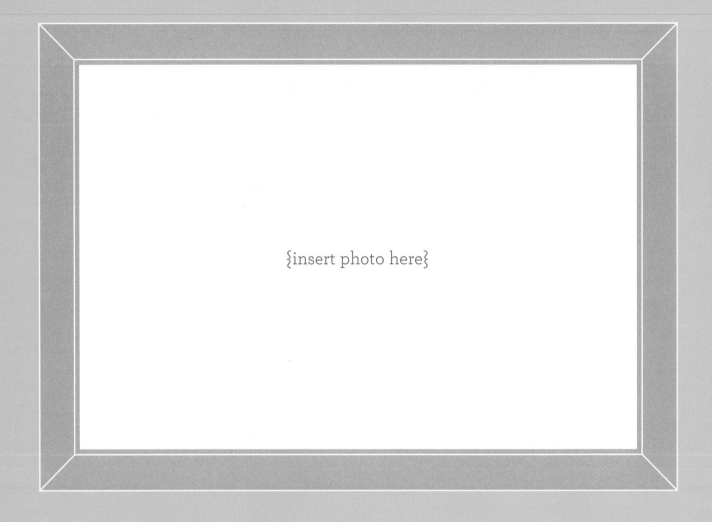

{insert photo here}

"The ornament of a house is
the friends who frequent it."

—RALPH WALDO EMERSON

Your visitors came bearing gifts. Some of the special presents
you received were:

_____

_____

_____

_____

_____

_____

Our favorite comments by your visitors:

_____

_____

_____

_____

_____

_____

"The best and most beautiful things in the world cannot be seen or even touched— they must be felt with the heart."

—HELEN KELLER

CELEBRATIONS

Name of the spiritual ceremony we celebrated:

_____

Place and date:

_____

On this special occasion, you wore:

_____

Friends and family who attended:

_____

_____

_____

_____

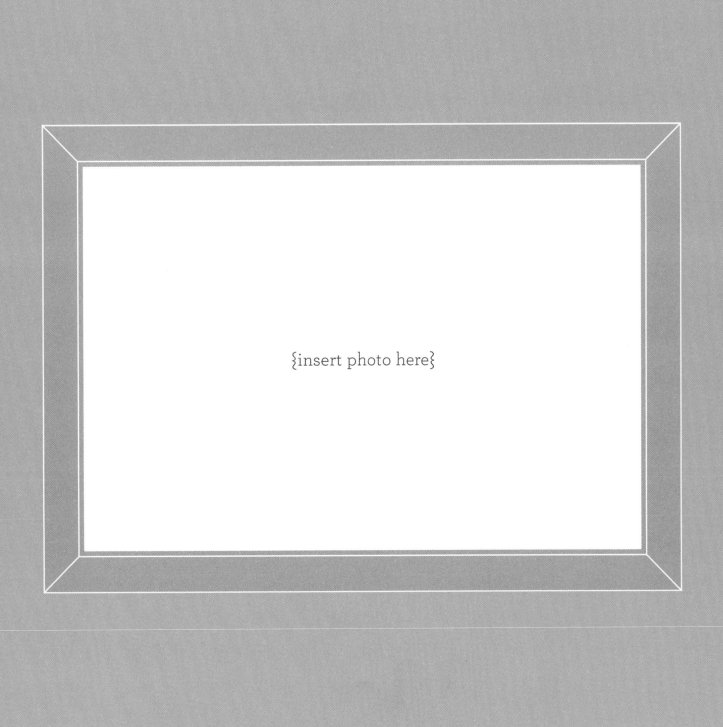

{insert photo here}

YOUR ASTROLOGICAL SIGN

Your astrological sign is:

_____

 Capricorn, The Goat:
December 22-January 19

 Aquarius, The Water Bearer:
January 20-February 18

 Pisces, The Fish:
February 19-March 20

 Aries, The Ram:
March 21-April 19

 Taurus, The Bull:
April 20-May 20

 Gemini, The Twins:
May 21-June 20

 Cancer, The Crab:
June 21-July 22

 Leo, The Lion:
July 23-August 22

 Virgo, The Virgin:
August 23-September 22

 Libra, The Scales:
September 23-October 22

 Scorpio, The Scorpion:
October 23-November 21

 Sagittarius, The Archer:
November 22-December 21

THE CHINESE ZODIAC

Your Chinese astrological sign is:

_____

 Rat
2020, 2008, 1996, 1984

 Ox
2021, 2009, 1997, 1985

 Tiger
2022, 2010, 1998, 1986

 Rabbit
2023, 2011, 1999, 1987

 Dragon
2024, 2012, 2000, 1988

 Snake
2025, 2013, 2001, 1989

 Horse
2026, 2014, 2002, 1990

 Goat
2027, 2015, 2003, 1991

 Monkey
2028, 2016, 2004, 1992

 Rooster
2029, 2017, 2005, 1993

 Dog
2018, 2006, 1994, 1982

 Pig
2019, 2007, 1995, 1983

YOUR BIRTHSTONE

Your birthstone is:

_____

January: Garnet

February: Amethyst

March: Aquamarine

April: Diamond, white sapphire

May: Emerald

June: Pearl, alexandrite

July: Ruby

August: Peridot, sardonyx

September: Sapphire

October: Opal, tourmaline

November: Topaz, citrine

December: Turquoise, zircon

YOUR BIRTHDAY FLOWER

Your birthday flower is:

_____

January: Carnation, snowdrop

February: Violet, primrose

March: Daffodil, jonquil

April: Daisy, sweet pea

May: Lily of the valley, hawthorn

June: Rose, honeysuckle

July: Larkspur, water lily

August: Gladiolus, poppy

September: Aster, morning glory

October: Cosmos

November: Chrysanthemum

December: Narcissus, holly

YOUR FIRST YEAR

Time does fly,
but in this chapter, we freeze
your precious first 12 months
for a sentimental reprise.

YOUR FIRST MONTH

{insert photo here}

You check in at _____ inches and _____ lbs.

Our favorite memories of this month:

_____

_____

_____

_____

_____

_____

_____

This month, you learned:

_____

_____

_____

_____

_____

_____

Your typical day:

_____

_____

_____

_____

_____

Your favorite thing to do:

_____

_____

_____

Places and people you visited:

_____

_____

_____

YOUR SECOND MONTH

{insert photo here}

You check in at _____ inches and _____ lbs.

Our favorite memories of this month:

_____

_____

_____

_____

_____

_____

This month, you learned:

_____

_____

_____

_____

_____

Your typical day:

_____

_____

_____

_____

_____

Your favorite thing to do:

_____

_____

_____

Places and people you visited:

_____

_____

_____

_____

YOUR THIRD MONTH

{insert photo here}

You check in at _____ inches and _____ lbs.

Our favorite memories of this month:

_____

_____

_____

_____

_____

This month, you learned:

_____

_____

_____

_____

_____

"There is no such thing in anyone's life as an unimportant day."

—ALEXANDER WOOLLCOTT

Your typical day:

_____
_____
_____
_____
_____
_____
_____

Your favorite thing to do:

_____
_____
_____
_____

Places and people you visited:

_____
_____
_____

YOUR FOURTH MONTH

{insert photo here}

You check in at _____ inches and _____ lbs.

Our favorite memories of this month:

_____

_____

_____

_____

_____

_____

_____

This month, you learned:

_____

_____

_____

_____

_____

_____

Your typical day:

_____

_____

_____

_____

_____

_____

Your favorite thing to do:

_____

_____

_____

_____

Places and people you visited:

_____

_____

_____

_____

YOUR FIFTH MONTH

{insert photo here}

You check in at _____ inches and _____ lbs.

Our favorite memories of this month:

_____

_____

_____

_____

_____

_____

This month, you learned:

_____

_____

_____

_____

_____

_____

Your typical day:

_____

_____

_____

_____

_____

_____

Your favorite thing to do:

_____

_____

_____

_____

Places and people you visited:

_____

_____

_____

_____

YOUR SIXTH MONTH

{insert photo here}

You check in at _____ inches and _____ lbs.

Our favorite memories of this month:

_____

_____

_____

_____

_____

_____

This month, you learned:

_____

_____

_____

_____

_____

_____

"We are happy when
we are growing."

—W. B. YEATS

Your typical day:

_____

_____

_____

_____

_____

Your favorite thing to do:

_____

_____

_____

_____

Places and people you visited:

_____

_____

_____

_____

"Love the moment, and the energy of that moment will spread beyond all boundaries."

—CORITA KENT

YOUR SEVENTH MONTH

{insert photo here}

You check in at _____ inches and _____ lbs.

Our favorite memories of this month:

_____

_____

_____

_____

_____

_____

This month, you learned:

_____

_____

_____

_____

_____

_____

Your typical day:

_____

_____

_____

_____

_____

_____

Your favorite thing to do:

_____

_____

_____

_____

Places and people you visited:

_____

_____

_____

_____

YOUR EIGHTH MONTH

{insert photo here}

You check in at _____ inches and _____ lbs.

Our favorite memories of this month:

_____
_____
_____
_____
_____
_____
_____

This month, you learned:

_____
_____
_____
_____
_____
_____

Your typical day:

_____

_____

_____

_____

_____

Your favorite thing to do:

_____

_____

_____

Places and people you visited:

_____

_____

_____

YOUR NINTH MONTH

{insert photo here}

You check in at _____ inches and _____ lbs.

Our favorite memories of this month:

_____

_____

_____

_____

_____

_____

_____

This month, you learned:

_____

_____

_____

_____

_____

_____

Your typical day:

_____

_____

_____

_____

_____

_____

Your favorite thing to do:

_____

_____

_____

_____

Places and people you visited:

_____

_____

_____

_____

"Enjoy the little things,
for one day you may
look back and realize
they were the big things."

—ROBERT BRAULT

YOUR TENTH MONTH

{insert photo here}

You check in at _____ inches and _____ lbs.

Our favorite memories of this month:

_____

_____

_____

_____

_____

_____

This month, you learned:

_____

_____

_____

_____

_____

Your typical day:

_____

_____

_____

_____

_____

_____

Your favorite thing to do:

_____

_____

_____

Places and people you visited:

_____

_____

_____

YOUR ELEVENTH MONTH

{insert photo here}

You check in at _____ inches and _____ lbs.

Our favorite memories of this month:

_____

_____

_____

_____

_____

_____

This month, you learned:

_____

_____

_____

_____

_____

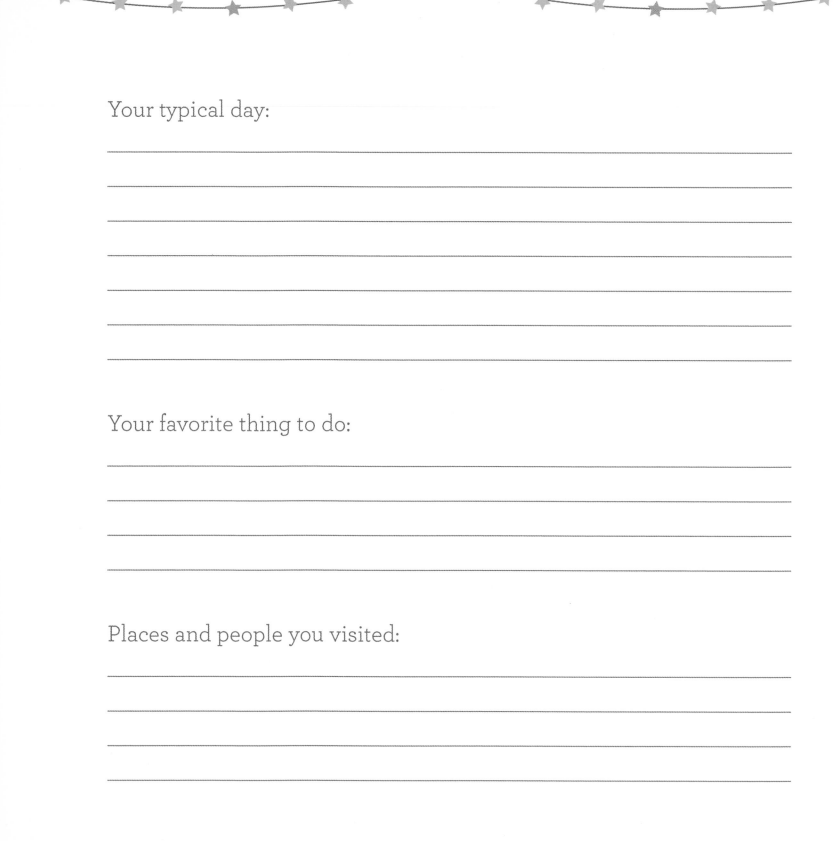

Your typical day:

_____

_____

_____

_____

_____

Your favorite thing to do:

_____

_____

_____

Places and people you visited:

_____

_____

_____

YOUR TWELFTH MONTH

{insert photo here}

You check in at _____ inches and _____ lbs.

Our favorite memories of this month:

_____
_____
_____
_____
_____
_____

This month, you learned:

_____
_____
_____
_____
_____
_____

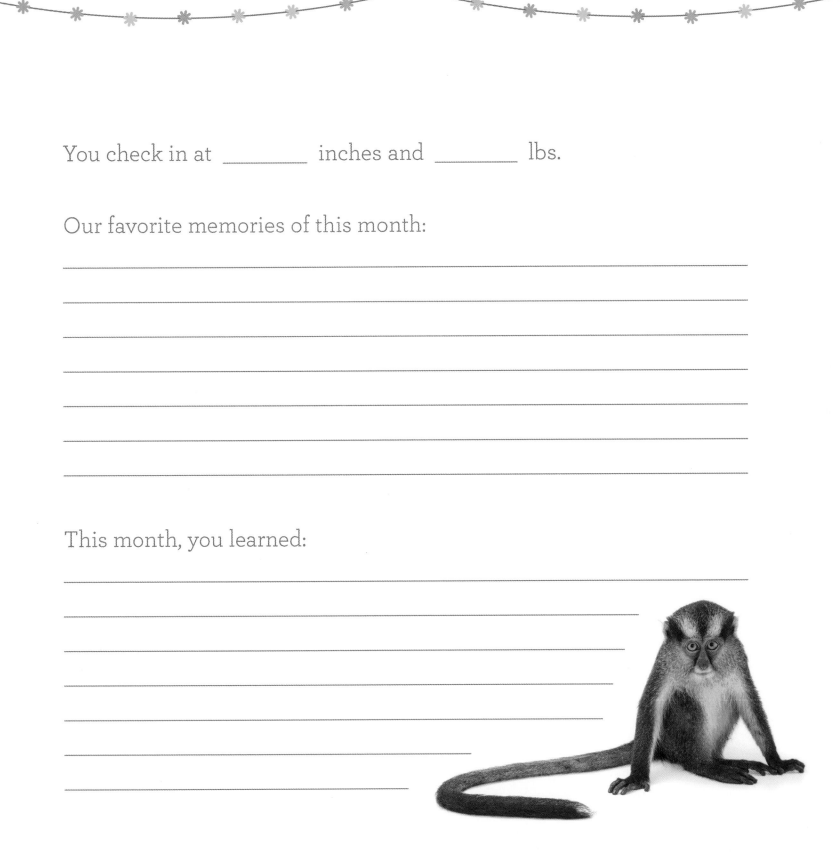

Your typical day:

_____

_____

_____

_____

_____

_____

Your favorite thing to do:

_____

_____

_____

Places and people you visited:

_____

_____

_____

"The greatest joy lies not in simply being, but in becoming."

—OPRAH WINFREY

YOUR 1ST BIRTHDAY PARTY

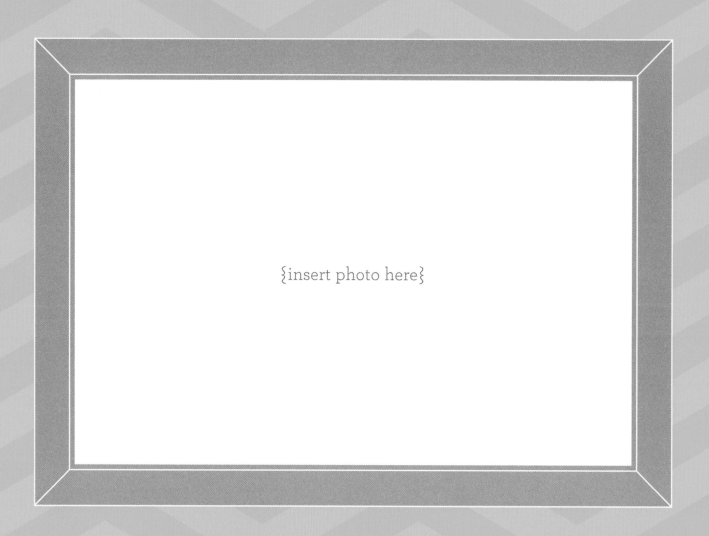

{insert photo here}

Who celebrated with you:

_____

_____

_____

_____

Your gifts included:

_____

_____

_____

_____

Favorite moments from your party:

_____

_____

_____

_____

_____

MEMORIES
&
MILESTONES

With each milestone that passes

you change and you grow.

We're so proud of all

you now do and now know.

BEDTIME

You started sleeping through the night on:

_____

Your favorite bedtime companions:

Bedtime rituals:

"Oh sleep! It is a gentle thing,
Beloved from pole to pole!"

—SAMUEL TAYLOR COLERIDGE

SMILES & LAUGHS

We first saw you smile on:

_____

You smiled because:

_____

Who saw your first smile:

_____

We first heard you laugh on:

_____

You laughed because:

_____

Who heard your first laugh:

_____

"Against the assault of laughter nothing can stand."

–MARK TWAIN

"I never lose sight of the fact
that just being is fun."

-KATHARINE HEPBURN

BATHTIME

You had your first bath on:

_____

Who gave you your bath:

_____

Your reaction was:

_____

Favorite tub toys:

_____

Favorite bath rituals:

_____

_____

_____

"We find delight in the beauty and happiness of children that makes the heart too big for the body."

—RALPH WALDO EMERSON

YOUR FIRST HAIRCUT

You had your first haircut on:

_____

Who gave you your haircut:

_____

Your reaction was:

_____

_____

_____

_____

_____

_____

_____

"Love is not a because,
it's a no matter what."

—JODI PICOULT

YOUR FIRST TOOTH

Your first tooth appeared:

_____

It was in the _____ part of your mouth.

Your favorite teething toy was:

_____

_____

Signs you gave us that your first tooth was on its way:

_____

_____

_____

You had _____ teeth by the end
of your first year.

"At any given moment
there are a thousand
things you can love."

–DAVID LEVITHAN

"All life is an experiment. The more experiments you make the better."

—RALPH WALDO EMERSON

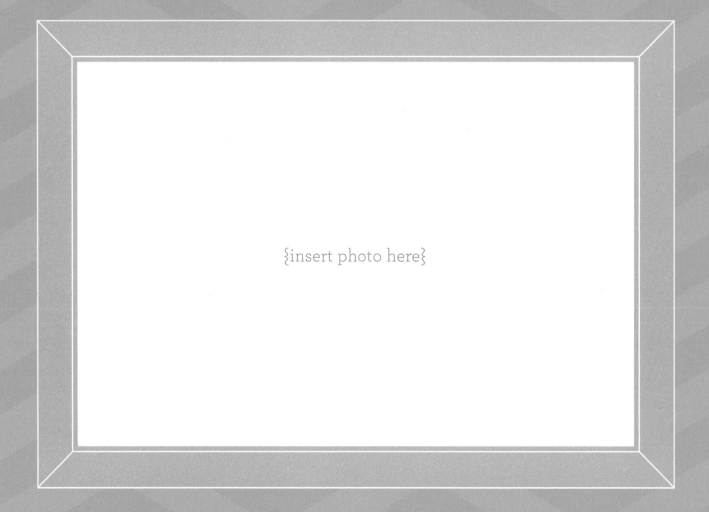

{insert photo here}

FOOD FIRSTS

You tried your first solid food on:

_____

The menu was:

_____

How you reacted:

_____

_____

Before long, some of your favorite foods were:

_____

You were not fond of:

_____

"We do not need magic to change the world, we carry all the power we need inside ourselves already: we have the power to imagine better."

—J. K. ROWLING

ON THE MOVE

You rolled over for the first time on:

_____

The first time you sat up by yourself was:

_____

You started crawling:

_____

You took your first steps:

_____

Your favorite places to explore were:

_____

_____

_____

"Always be on the watch for the coming of wonders."

—E. B. WHITE, *CHARLOTTE'S WEB*

YOUR FIRST WORDS

You started babbling on:

_____

The first word you spoke was:

_____

When and where you said your first word:

_____

Before long, you added these words to your vocabulary:

_____

_____

Other ways you communicated with us:

_____

_____

Parents' Names Around the World

LANGUAGE	MOM	DAD
Danish	mor	far
Finnish	äiti	isä
French	maman	papa
Hawaiian	makuahine or māmā	makua kāne or makua
Hindi	माता maa-taa or amma	पिता pi-taa or bapp
Indonesian	ibu	ayah
Italian	mamma	babbo or papa
Japanese	お母さん okaasan or haha	お父さん otōsan or chichi
Mandarin	母亲 mā or mǔqīn	父亲 bà or fùqīn
Swahili	mama	baba
Turkish	anne	baba
Welsh	mam	tad

PLAYTIME!

You had your first play date on:

_____

Your first friends were:

_____

_____

_____

_____

You loved to play:

_____

_____

_____

_____

_____

"Be silly. Be honest.
Be kind."

—RALPH WALDO EMERSON

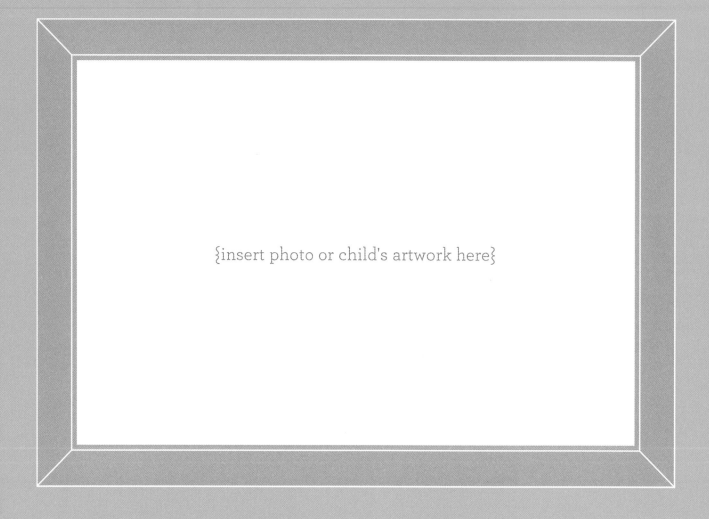

{insert photo or child's artwork here}

"The power of imagination
makes us infinite."

–JOHN MUIR

YOUR ARTWORK

You made this drawing on:

_____

It looks like:

_____

To make this drawing you used:

_____

_____

_____

How you like to show your creative side:

_____

_____

_____

"What is a family, after all, except memories?—haphazard and precious as the contents of a catchall drawer in the kitchen."

—JOYCE CAROL OATES, *WE WERE THE MULVANEYS*

ROAD TRIPS

You took your first road trip on:

_____

You went to:

_____

You were accompanied by:

_____

People, places, and things you saw there:

_____

_____

_____

_____

_____

"My favorite thing is to
go where I've never been."

—DIANE ARBUS

{insert photo here}

HOLIDAYS

The first major holiday you celebrated was:

_____

You celebrated it with:

_____

You wore:

_____

Favorite memories from your first holidays:

_____

_____

_____

_____

_____

YOUR ACHIEVEMENTS

You've grown and learned so much! We want to remember these other achievements that made you, and us, so proud.

_____

_____

_____

_____

_____

_____

_____

_____

_____

_____

_____

_____

_____

"We are not yet what we shall be, but we are growing toward it, the process is not yet finished ..."

—MARTIN LUTHER

"If you are interested in something, no matter what it is, go at it full speed. Embrace it with both arms, hug it, love it and above all become passionate about it. Lukewarm is no good."

—ROALD DAHL

LOOK AT ME GROW

1 Year Old

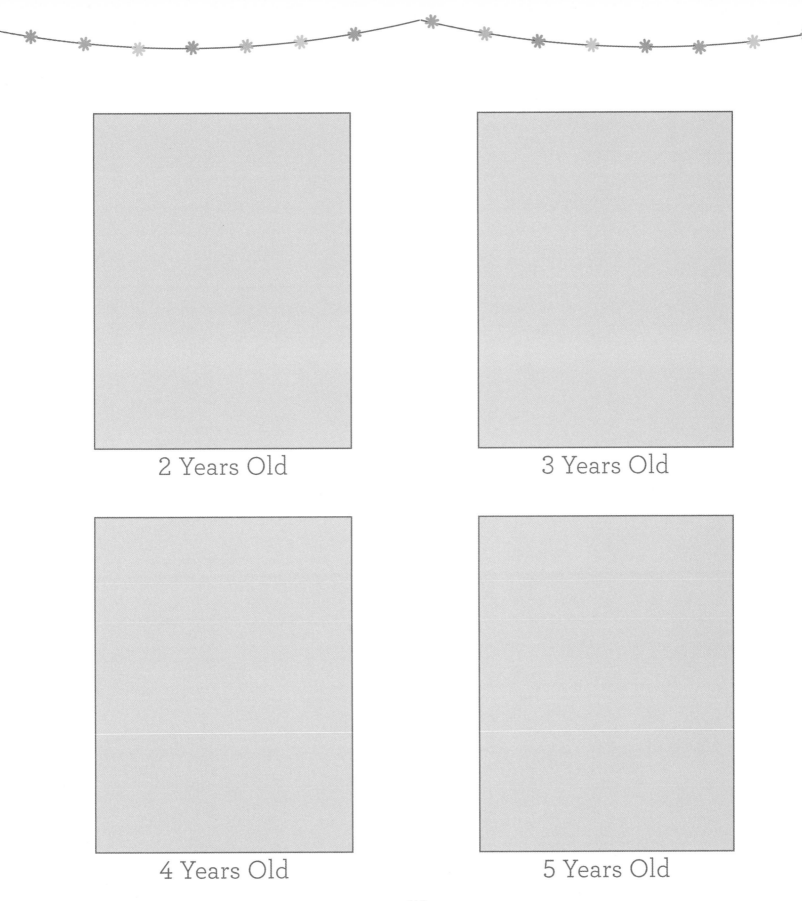

2 Years Old

3 Years Old

4 Years Old

5 Years Old

Kindergarten

First Grade

Second Grade

Third Grade

Fourth Grade

Fifth Grade

Sixth Grade

Seventh Grade

Eighth Grade

Ninth Grade

Tenth Grade

Eleventh Grade

Twelfth Grade

"Growth itself contains
the germ of happiness."

—PEARL S. BUCK

WISHES FOR YOU NOW...

Dear Little One,

_____

_____

_____

_____

_____

_____

_____

_____

_____

_____

_____

"There are only two lasting bequests we can hope to give our children. One of these is roots, the other wings."

—HODDING CARTER

...AND LATER

Parents, write down the wishes you'd like your child to read on his/her 18th birthday. Then fold over the page and tape it closed.

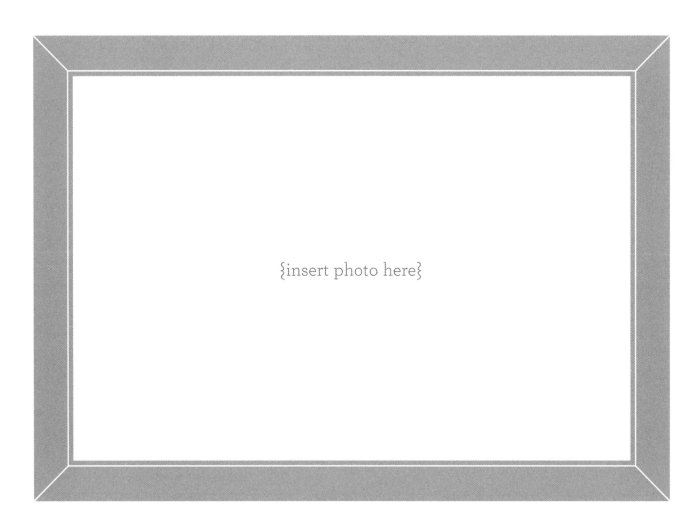

{insert photo here}

> "Never underestimate the power of dreams and the influence of the human spirit. The potential for greatness lives within each of us."
>
> —WILMA RUDOLPH

_____

_____

_____

_____

_____

_____

_____

_____

_____

_____

_____

MILESTONE INDEX

Illustrations Credits

PHOTO ARK

About the Photo Ark

Many of the animal portraits in this book come from the Photo Ark, a multiyear National Geographic project with a simple goal: to capture portraits of the world's species before they disappear and to inspire people everywhere to care about the extinction crisis. Each image is a visual connection between animals and people who can help protect them. With ingenuity, wit, and a serious midwestern work ethic, Joel Sartore has made studio-quality images of more than 6,500 species to date—nearly half the world's captive species—and is taking more photographs all the time. Many of the animals he portrays live in the world's zoos and aquariums, institutions dedicated to preserving and caring for species of all kinds. The Photo Ark is the largest archive of its kind, and growing. With your support it will become an even more amazing resource for future generations and a reminder of a world worth saving. To learn more about what you can do, visit *nationalgeographic.com/photoark.*

1 month

2 months

3 months

FIRST Tooth

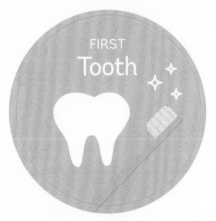

I ♥ MOM

I ♥ MOM

FIRST Word

ABC

4 months

5 months

6 months

FIRST Bath

I ♥ DAD

I ♥ DAD

FIRST Haircut

7 months

8 months

9 months

FIRST
Play Date

I ♥ GRANDMA

I ♥ GRANDMA

FIRST
Food

10 months

11 months

12 months

FIRST
Steps

I ♥ GRANDPA

I ♥ GRANDPA

FIRST
Road Trip